中国科幻小说精选·中英对照

THE MAGIC FLUTE OF TIANJIALIN

雪山魔笛

童恩正 著
温绍贤 译
[英] 蒂娜·巴莱 审校

科学普及出版社
·北 京·

图书在版编目（CIP）数据

雪山魔笛：中英对照/童恩正著；温绍贤译．—北京：科学普及出版社，2014.6

（中国科幻小说精选）

ISBN 978-7-110-08377-2

Ⅰ．①雪… Ⅱ．①童… ②温… Ⅲ．①英语—汉语—对照读物 ②儿童文学—科学幻想小说—作品集—中国—当代 Ⅳ．①H319.4：I

中国版本图书馆CIP数据核字(2014)第096623号

出版人	苏 青
责任编辑	单 亭 张 莉
封面设计	银搏时代
责任校对	王勤杰
责任印制	张建农

出　　版	科学普及出版社
发　　行	科学普及出版社发行部
地　　址	北京市海淀区中关村南大街16号
邮　　编	100081
发行电话	010-62173865
传　　真	010-62179148
网　　址	http://www.cspbooks.com.cn

开　　本	880mm×1230mm　1/32
字　　数	38千字
印　　张	3
印　　数	1—5000册
版　　次	2014年8月第1版
印　　次	2014年8月第1次印刷
印　　刷	北京盛通印刷股份有限公司
书　　号	ISBN 978-7-110-08377-2 / H·209
定　　价	16.00元

（凡购买本社图书，如有缺页、倒页、脱页者，本社发行部负责调换）

CONTENTS

目录

关于雪山魔笛的故事以及喜马拉雅山区富有震惊性的新闻，我想你们已经知道了。然而整个事件经历的过程，以及它带给我们这些当事人的紧张、悬念和兴奋，却不是三言两语所能概括的。在这里，我将根据我的工作日记，详细地将在这远离人世的雪山深谷里发生的一切，从头到尾讲给你们听。

You must have heard of the Magic Flute of Tianjialin and of the shocking events that took place in Himalayan valley. However, the details of the whole story and the tension, suspense and excitement we all experienced cannot be summed up in a few words. Now I am going to tell you all that happened up there, far from any human habitation, as I recorded it in my diary.

在天嘉林寺的废墟上

我们这一支小小的考古调查队在天嘉林寺的废墟上进行试掘，已经整整三个月了。天嘉林寺位于喜马拉雅山支脉康格山东麓的坡顶上，面对风景如画的安林湖。在康格山的这一地区，西、北两面是高耸入云的大山，冰封雪积，亘古不化；山腰云雾缭绕，变幻莫测。东南方则是深陷的峡谷，灰白色的花岗石壁立千仞，寸草不生，狰狞可怖。唯有在安林湖周围数十千米的缓坡上，景色完全不同，橡树、赤杨、山毛榉、杉树，构成一片繁茂的原始森林。熊、鹿、猴子、狐狸、野兔、山羊、麝猫等动物，栖息其间。湖畔绿草如茵，溪流潺潺，雪白的天鹅悠然地游过水面，看来真像一座与世隔绝的天堂。

在古代，天嘉林寺曾经是红教的圣地之一。在那繁荣的日子里，山间崎岖的小道上朝香拜佛的人络绎不绝。到17世纪中期，在当时黄教与红教剧烈的争权斗争中，天嘉林寺被支持黄教的厄鲁特人所焚毁。随着时间的流逝，

STRANGE FIND IN THE TEMPLE RUINS

Our small archaeological survey team had been at work for three months doing test excavations among the ruins of Tianjialin Temple. This temple is situated on the eastern lower slopes of Mount Kangga, a spur of the Himalayas overlooking the picturesque Lake Anlin. North and west of Mt. Kangga are towering mountain peaks scored by permanent glaciers and swathed in ever-changing cloud and mist. To the southeast deep gorges with sombre granite walls plunge to a depth of seven or eight thousand feet. Not a blade of grass grows in that forbidding terrain. But around Lake Anlin there is a very different scene. Sloping up and away from the lake for about scores of kilometres is a belt of primeval forest of oak, red poplar, beech and fir inhabited by bears, deer, monkeys, foxes, hares, goats and civets. On the lake shore is a carpet of green grass, and streams flow through it into the lake on whose surface a flotilla of white swans glides serenely. The whole area is a paradise completely cut off from the outside world.

In ancient times Tianjialin Temple was the holy shrine of the Red Sect. In its heyday a continuous stream of pilgrims made their way to it along rugged mountain paths. In the middle of the 17th century the Yellow Sect and the Red Sect were locked in a fierce struggle for power and the temple was burnt down by the Eruta people who supported the Yellow Sect. As time went by, the ancient temple in the remote mountains

这深山古刹逐渐为人所遗忘，它的残垣断壁几乎完全埋没在荒烟蔓草之中，只有那幸存的鎏金尖塔寂寞地映着落日的余晖。

在红教的历史中，天嘉林寺似乎笼罩着一层神秘的色彩。其中流传最广的传说，是有关最后一届高僧拉布山嘉措的事迹。据说他精通巫术，能降魔伏鬼。他有一支魔笛，可以召唤山精现形，前来听他讲经。作为一个考古学家，我自然知道过去西藏的农奴主阶级惯于利用喇嘛的迷信活动欺骗人民，为他们的统治服务，因此在一般情况下，是不会认真地对待这类传说的。但是关于拉布山嘉措的“魔笛”和他召唤山精的故事，在 17 世纪前期曾经被很多拜访过天嘉林寺的人所目睹，他们之中有官吏、商人和旅行家，如果说这些人的记载全属虚构，那似乎也不合情理。因此，每天的工作结束以后，我坐在帐篷前面的篝火旁，看着被夕阳染成红色的雪峰、晶莹清澈的湖水、青翠茂密的森林以及天嘉林寺黑色的废墟，我的心中就会浮现出一种奇异的幻想，如果这里的湖山能够说话，在缓缓流逝的历

was forgotten; its jagged walls were shrouded in mist and trailing plants and only the gold-plated pinnacle of the pagoda stood out, glittering desolately in the setting sun.

In the history of the Red Sect, Tianjialin Temple seems to have been a subject of mystery and wonder. The best-known legend tells of the last Senior Monk, Lhabushan Jiaqu, who was said to be deeply versed in witchcraft and able to subdue demons and ghosts. He had a magic flute which, so the story goes, could summon the mountain goblins to his presence, where they would appear before him and listen to him expounding Buddhist texts. As an archaeologist I knew that in the past the serf-owners of Tibet did not hesitate to make use of the Lamaist superstitions to delude the people and keep them in subjection. So, generally speaking, I didn't take legends of this sort very seriously. However, in the early l7th century many people, including officials, merchants and travellers who visited Tianjialin Temple claimed to have seen Lhabushan Jiaqu's magic flute and the mountain goblins it summoned to his presence. It seemed unlikely that all these records were fabrications. For this reason, every day when the day's work was over and I was sitting by the campfire in front of the tent, looking at the snowy peaks red in the sunset, the clear lake, the green and thick forest and the dark temple ruins, strange fantasies would come to my mind. If only the lake and the mountains could speak, what stories forgotten by

史长河之中，它将向我们倾诉多少被人遗忘的故事呢？

在三个月的工作中，我们已经从废墟里找到了很多宝贵的经卷雕板、手抄文献、宗教法器，临摹了残存的壁画。由于红教在西藏流传的历史非常悠久，保留了较多的原始巫教的成分，因此这批资料对于研究西藏古代的神话、民族、历史等方面，都有重要的参考价值。这样，我们的工作就比预期要延长一些，至少要拖到七月下旬。过去在藏族曾经这样形容过本地区的交通情况："正二三，雪封山；四五六，淋得哭；七八九，正好走；十冬腊，学狗爬。"这就是说，从十月开始，地面的积雪已经很深，旅行的人只能像狗爬似地越过没膝的深雪。如果是在过去，我们老早就应当在大雪封山以前赶回拉萨去了。然而现在我们的国家已经用先进的装备保证了调查队的安全，我们每天都和在拉萨的大本营保持无线电联系，全天候喷气式直升机随时可以来支援我们，所以季节的变换并没有引起我们过多地考虑。

天嘉林寺剩下的比较完整的部分，除了经塔以外，还

the people they could tell in the endless and gradual flow of history!

During our three months of work we had found many valuable blocks of stone with passages of sutras cut on them, some hand-written documents and some religious musical instruments. We had also made copies of what was left of the murals. The Red Sect had a very long history in Tibet so its writings contained many of the elements of primitive sorcery. These materials were, therefore, of importance for research into ancient mythology, nationalities and history of Tibet, and as such, our work took longer than we had planned, at least stretching into late October. Tibetans have traditionally described their land's traffic conditions like this: “In January, February and March the snow blocks the mountain passes, and in April, May and June there are rainstorms; it is the best time to travel in July, August and September, but snow gets deeper and deeper in October, November and December and people have to crawl on the snow like dogs”. In the past we would have had to hurry back to Lhasa before the snow had sealed the mountain passes, but now with modern facilities our safety was assured. We were in daily radio contact with Lhasa and the all-weather jet helicopter could reach us whenever necessary. The change of season, therefore, had no particular impact on us.

The relatively well-preserved parts of Tianjialin Temple were the vihara tower and the central lectorium. The building

有中央的经堂。这里的屋宇虽然已经残破，但是还没有完全倒坍。经堂里的佛像、神龛、经鼓等都大致无缺。很自然的，我们工作的重点，也就放到了这里。

经堂的中央，是红教的主神之一降魔天尊的塑像。它的涂金彩绘已经剥落，肢体残缺，露出了泥胎，不过轮廓仍然清楚，瞪目咧嘴，手持法轮，脚踏妖魔，形象十分恐怖。无论如何，这座塑像代表了较早期的红教艺术的某些特征，所以我们仍然对它进行了测绘、照相。

进行这项工作的，是测绘员索伦和某大学派到我们这里来进行毕业实习的冯元。索伦这小伙子是调查队的活跃人物，头脑灵，反应快，生性诙谐，哪里有了他，哪里就少不了笑声。冯元是一个十分聪明伶俐的姑娘，除了参加业务工作外，还兼任调查队的护士，很受大家的欢迎。平日这两个青年人别出心裁的玩笑，往往给调查队的生活带来不少乐趣。

幽暗的经堂里被闪光灯所照亮，这是索伦和冯元结束了绘图，在给佛像摄影了。等到他们从各个角度拍完照片以后，我听到他们两人开始了一场议论。

was dilapidated but it had not collapsed completely. The figures of Buddha, the shrine and the drums in the lectorium were mostly well preserved. Naturally these formed the focal point of our work here.

In the middle of the lectorium was a statue of Buddha Subduing Demons, one of the main Buddhas of the Red Sect. Its coat of gold paint had peeled off and its incomplete limbs and trunk were revealed in their original unpainted clay. But its outline and some details were still clearly defined: it had fierce eyes and a grinning mouth; it was holding a prayer wheel and trampling on a demon with its foot. It was a fearful looking thing, but it represented certain features of the art of the early period of the Red Sect, so we surveyed it and photographed it.

The work was done by Solon, the surveyor, and Feng Yuan, a university student doing her graduation field work. Solon, the young guy, was the live wire of the team: he was quick-witted, quick in action and something of a humorist. There would always be laughter wherever he was working. Feng Yuan was a very intelligent young woman who also looked after the group in addition to her professional work. We all liked her. She and Solon went in for a good deal of wise-cracking and joking that cheered us all up.

The gloomy lectorium was suddenly brilliantly lit with a flash. Solon and Feng Yuan had finished making their notes on the Buddha figure and were photographing it. When they had done this from various angles I heard them arguing.

“外部的工作已经完了，让我们把它的内脏掏出来看看。”索伦说。

“别干傻事，这是破坏文物。”冯元不同意。

“说不定它肚子里藏着什么宝贝。”

“你想发洋财是不是？”

“不是开玩笑，你看这儿，不是像有一扇小门吗？”

“咦，真是有点道理。”冯元回过头来喊我，“老王，你快过来看看！”

我和精通古藏语的次仁旺堆正在研究一块残存的壁画上的咒语，听到冯元的喊声，立即放下手边的工作，走过去一看，结果证明索伦的观察是正确的。在这尊佛像腹部的中央，有一块长方形的痕迹，在最初它可能完全被腰带的装饰所掩盖，现在由于表面的涂料脱落，现出了缝隙。根据我过去勘察喇嘛庙的经验，可以断定这是修建佛像时故意留下的一个小龛，是喇嘛们保存圣物用的。

我用手铲轻轻地撬开泥胎，露出了一扇活门。打开活门以后，果然发现了一个很深的方龛，里面放着一个深褐

"As we've finished with its outside, let's take it to pieces and see what's inside," said Solon.

"Don't be crazy! You can't destroy cultural relics!" protested Feng Yuan.

"But there might be some hidden treasure in its belly."

"You're just hoping to make a fortune out of it, aren't you?"

"I'm not joking. Look, doesn't that look like some sort of opening?"

"Good lord, yes, you're right." Feng Yuan turned and called to me, "Wang, come quick and have a look!"

I was studying an incantation on a surviving piece of mural with Ciren Wangdui, an expert in ancient Tibetan, when I heard Feng Yuan call. I immediately stopped my work and went over and found Solon's observation was correct: in the middle of the belly of the Buddha was a rectangular mark. Originally it would have been completely covered by the painted waistband but now, with the paint gone, cracks had appeared. From past experience of surveying Lama temples I knew it could be a small niche intentionally made during the original construction of the Buddha. Such niches were used by the lamas for preserving holy objects.

I carefully levered out the rectangle of clay with a trowel and revealed a valve. When the valve was opened we found that in it there was indeed a deep, square niche. In the niche

色铜盒。

我们小心谨慎地将铜盒取出，拂去灰尘以后，发现上面满布精美的莲花图案，就它本身而言，堪称一件珍贵的艺术品。盒盖上贴着封条，上面写着“唵嘛呢叭咪吽”六字真言，还盖有法印。

我们怀着强烈的好奇心打开了盒盖，里面放着一支人骨制的笛子，一卷羊皮纸的手抄本，上面写着古老的藏文。

这一切是什么意思呢?

was a dark brown copper box.

With great care we took the box out. We wiped away the dust and found that it was covered all over with delicate incised lotus patterns: the box itself was an exquisite work of art. There was a paper strip stuck on the lid bearing six charm characters and a religious seal chop.

Prompted by strong curiosity, we opened it. Inside lay a flute made of human bone and some parchment with writing in the ancient Tibetan language.

What did it all mean?

雪地上的脚印

你见过西藏高原雪山冰湖的月夜吗？你能想象那种肃穆、含蓄、神秘的气氛吗？

当一轮明月高悬天际，用它那清澈的光芒普照大地时，银光闪闪的群山、盖着雪冠的森林以及像明镜一样的湖泊，似乎都凝结在一层透明的薄雾之中，坠入了梦境。在白天看来如此美丽的景色，在月光下却呈现出另外一种气氛，好像使人进入了一种久已被人忘怀的童话世界。

然而在今天晚上，调查队里却没有人注意到这美妙的夜景。次仁旺堆正在帐篷里的灯下细心研究着铜盒里的手抄文书，我们其余的人坐在旁边，屏住气息等待着这谜底的揭晓。

外面是一片深山里特有的寂静。偶尔一阵微风吹过，就连周围云杉上掉下的雪块“簌簌”的声音，也清晰可闻。

次仁旺堆手中的放大镜慢慢地在羊皮纸上移动。虽然

FOOTPRINTS IN THE SNOW

Have you ever seen a moonlit lake on the Tibetan plateau below the great glaciers? Can you imagine the mysterious, spooky, other-worldly atmosphere of such a scene?

The moon hangs high in the sky silvering everything on earth—the mountains, the forest with its turban of snow, the mirror-like lake: a transparent gauze of mist transforms reality into a dream. The scenery, spectacularly beautiful by day, by moon-light becomes a fairy landscape which people have had no chance to see for ages.

However, none of us gave a thought to the wonderful scenery that night. Ciren Wangdui was carefully studying the hand-written text from the copper box under the light in the tent. We sat round him, waiting with bated breath for the answer to the riddle.

Outside was the dead silence peculiar to remote mountains. An occasional breath of wind crept by and we could clearly hear even the rustling of snow falling to the ground from the dragon spruces round the camp.

The magnifying glass in Ciren Wangdui's hand was moving

他是国内知名的研究佛教史和古藏文的专家，但是这份文件经过了两百多年的岁月，墨迹已经褪色，加上在字句之间还穿插有一些巫术符号和已经失传的红教的术语，所以看上去十分吃力。

终于，次仁旺堆看完了最后一行，他抬起头来，习惯性地推推滑到鼻梁上的眼镜，脸上出现了一种困惑之色。

“这是天嘉林寺毁灭的前夕一个喇嘛留下的记载，”他慢慢地说，“根据这一记载，保存在铜盒里的人骨笛，应该就是拉布山嘉措大师的魔笛。”

“什么？”好几个声音同时发出了惊呼。

“是的，这就是那支传说中的魔笛。”次仁旺堆又重复了一次，“这个喇嘛对于魔笛的作用是深信不疑的，他之所以要写下这份文书，就是警告后世得到这支魔笛的人，千万不可将它吹响，特别不可在黑夜吹响，因为太阳落山以后，正是山精活动的时候，只要听到笛声，他们马上就会出现……”

索伦扑哧一声笑了出来，做了一个鬼脸，惹得坐在帐

slowly across the parchment. He was China's leading expert on Buddhist history and the ancient Tibetan language, but it was difficult for him to decipher the words because the ink had faded in more than 200 years. In addition, there were some symbols of witchcraft and some religious terms of the Red Sect which were not familiar from older Tibetan texts.

Finally he finished reading the last line. He raised his head, pushed his glasses back with his habitual gesture and sat looking perplexed.

"It is an account hidden away by a lama on the eve of the destruction of the temple," he said slowly. "According to it, the flute made of human bone kept in the copper box is the magic flute of the Great Master Lhabushan Jiaqu."

"What?" we all exclaimed in amazement.

"Yes, it is the magic flute of the legend," Ciren Wangdui repeated. "This lama firmly believed it was a magic flute. That is why he wrote this document to warn later generations that who ever got the flute must in no circumstances play it, especially at night, for after sunset the demons and goblins would come out and would immediately appear on hearing the flute played…"

Solon snorted in disbelief and pulled a face, which made

篷口的冯元也笑了。我知道他们都觉得次仁旺堆的脸色过于严肃，似乎在讨论什么科学问题。

老实的次仁旺堆没有理会两个青年人的嘲笑，仍然继续说下去："写下这份文书的喇嘛本人，就曾经亲眼目睹过拉布山嘉措用魔笛召唤山精的情景。他发下了红教中最重的誓言，是证明他所说的全是事实。现在我把这几句翻译给你们听：

'其时雪积满地，冰湖如镜，万籁俱寂，山林沉睡。拉布山嘉措大师端坐诵经，吹笛作法，山精鬼怪，接踵前来，僧俗诸众，合十膜拜。共叹佛法无边，神灵常在……'"

又是一个目击者的证词！我知道庄严的誓言对于红教的喇嘛具有何等的约束力，如果他确实没有亲眼看见这种怪现象的话，他是绝对不敢发誓的。这时我所熟悉的有关拉布山嘉措召唤山精的传说，一桩桩又出现在脑际，难道这仅仅是一些迷信的传说吗？

我从铜盒中取出这支笛子，再次将它仔细地观察了一

Feng Yuan, who was sitting at the entrance of the tent, giggle. I knew they thought Ciren Wangdui looked too seriously, as though he was discussing a scientific problem.

Ciren Wangdui, an honest person, paid no attention to the two young people's sneer and continued equably, "The lama who wrote this paper had seen with his own eyes the scenes in which Lhabushan Jiaqu used his flute to summon the mountain goblins. He made the most serious oath of the Red Sect to prove that all what he said was true. Now let me translate these few lines for you:

'At the time, the ground was covered with thick snow and the frozen lake was like a mirror. Silence reigned supreme and the forest was fast asleep. Great Master Lhabushan Jiaqu sat up straight chanting a sutra. Then he played the flute and the magic began to work. And then the mountain goblins, demons and ghosts came one after another, in succession. The monks and laymen present all clasped their hands in worship of him and praised the boundless power of Buddha and the eternal existence of deities ...'"

It was the testimony of yet another eyewitness! I knew a solemn oath would have a great binding force upon a lama of the Red Sect: if he had not actually seen such strange phenomena, himself, he would not have dared to swear. At the moment the legends so familiar to me nagged at my thoughts: were they really only superstitious legends?

I took the flute out of the copper box and carefully examined

番。这明显是用人的胫骨制成的，两端镶嵌着银饰。在旧社会喇嘛的法器中，人骨笛是常见的东西。除了这一支笛子制作得特别精致以外，我确实也看不出有什么特别之处。

次仁旺堆似乎看透了我的心思，他轻轻地说："老王，我始终觉得，在这支笛子里，可能隐藏着一桩什么秘密。"

我没有回答，我在沉思。

帐篷里又响起了冯元清脆的笑声："次仁旺堆，我看你是佛经读多了，着了迷。难道你真的相信有什么魔笛，有什么山精？"

次仁旺堆摇摇头："我当然不会迷信。但是这里面是不是会有其他的原因、其他的道理呢？你们看这支笛子，吹口的部分已经磨损，无疑是多次使用过的，如果它吹响以后而没有效果，拉布山嘉措能够那样受人崇拜？"

冯元不以为然地说："他骗人的嘛！"

"可是有那么多人亲眼看见过的。"

"那只能说他骗术高明。"冯元调皮地说，"又回到老问题上来了，难道你准备用迷信的理由来解释？"

it again. It was apparently made of human shinbone with silver inlays at both ends. In the old society, human bone was a popular material for the religious musical instruments used by the lamas. Indeed, I did not see anything extraordinary in this flute apart from its particularly exquisite workmanship.

Ciren Wangdui seemed to see into my mind and said softly, "Wang, I would rather think this flute may be the key to some secret."

I made no answer as I was pondering possibilities.

Feng Yuan's clear and melodious laughter broke into my concentration: "Comrade Ciren Wangdui, I think you've read too many Buddhist sutras and you're spellbound by them. Do you really believe in the 'magic flute' or 'mountain goblins'?"

Ciren Wangdui shook his head, "I'm not superstitious. But are there any other causes or reasons? Please look at this flute, look – here – round the blowing holes do you see? – there are signs of wear. That shows it was used repeatedly. If Lhabushan Jiaqu had played it with no effect, would people have worshipped him as they did?"

Feng Yuan was not convinced and said, "He deceived people."

"But many people claim that they actually saw what happened."

"That only means he was very clever with his tricks," retorted Feng Yuan naughtily. "Now you're back at the original question: are you really willing to accept a supernatural explanation?"

次仁旺堆推推眼镜："在旧社会，特别是在落后的西藏农奴制社会里，当人们还没有掌握大自然的奥妙，还不可能了解它的规律时，很多科学的现象都被披上了迷信的外衣，并且被统治阶级有意歪曲来为他们的利益服务。我认为魔笛的问题，就可能属于这种性质。"

我觉得次仁旺堆的话是有道理的，但是我还没有来得及开口，索伦就从我手里接过笛子，笑着插嘴了："你们俩别争了，我认为最好的办法，就是立刻吹响这支魔笛。现在正是夜晚，万籁俱寂，山林沉睡，一切条件都和传说相符合。如果笛声真的招来了山精，那就证明拉布山嘉措确实是佛法无边，让我们向他致敬；如果啥事也没有，那就证明这种传说只是一个骗局。而我们的次仁旺堆也上了当。一切让实践来回答吧！"

于是他将笛子举到唇边。次仁旺堆举起一只手来，似乎想要阻止他，但是索伦已经深深地吸了一口气，将笛子吹响了。

这笛子发出一种低沉的、呜呜的声音，与我们平日听

Ciren Wangdui pushed his glasses back and said, “In the old society, particularly in Tibet’s backward society of serfdom, many scientific phenomena were intentionally distorted and given superstitious trappings and were exploited by the ruling class to serve their own interests, as the people at that time were ignorant and had no understanding of the secrets and the laws of nature. I’m of the opinion that these facts may have some bearing on the legends surrounding the flute.”

I found Ciren Wangdui’s words reasonable. However, before I could speak Solon whisked the flute from my hand, saying with a smile:

“Oh, do stop arguing. I think the best way is to play the thing right now. It’s night-time now. It says in the parchment there ‘Silence reigned supreme and the forest was fast asleep’. Conditions are just right. If the flute brings ‘mountain goblins’ to us, then that will prove that Lhabushan Jiaqu really possessed ‘boundless power of Buddha’. In that case we must pay homage to him; if nothing happens, then we shall know that the whole thing was nothing but a swindle. And that would mean that even our Comrade Ciren Wangdui was fooled. Everything should be put to the test.”

So saying, he put the flute to his lips. Ciren Wangdui raised one hand, probably trying to stop him, but he had taken a deep breath and blown into the flute.

The sound was low and deep, with a hooting quality to it,

惯了的笛声毫无共同之处，更像是从人类喉咙深处发出的呼喊，在这寂静的夜空里，听起来有一种粗犷、原始的感觉。

索伦吹了一阵以后，停了下来，意味深长地望着次仁旺堆笑笑。

帐篷里没有人说话，周围仍然是深沉的寂静。

“也许吹一次不行吧，我可以吹三次。”索伦向冯元伸伸舌头，又一次吹响了笛子。

笛声延续了一两分钟之久，但是什么事也没有发生。

于是索伦长长地吹了第三次，低沉的、呜呜的声音，再一次在夜空中回响。

笛声停止以后，帐篷里仍然悄无声息。但是不知道是什么原因，每一个人都感到了一种紧张的期待的气氛。

索伦放下了笛子，满脸都是揶揄的笑容，他刚要向次仁旺堆说点什么，但是当他的视线接触到冯元的时候，却突然怔住了。

我们几乎同时都发现了冯元异常的神态，片刻之前还

completely unlike any normal flute notes. It was as if the cry of a human wrung from deep in the throat; in the still night air it was primitive, atavistic.

Solon stopped and looked at Ciren Wangdui with a meaning smile.

No one in the tent spoke; there was still dead silence around.

"Maybe once is not enough. I will try three times." Solon put out his tongue at Feng Yuan and lifted the flute to his lips again.

He blew again for about two minutes, but nothing happened.

Then he did it a third time for a longer time. The haunting sound echoed again in the night sky.

When he stopped there was nothing but silence in the camp. Without knowing why, we all felt tense and expectant.

Solon put down the flute, grinning derisively. He was about to say something to Ciren Wangdui when his glance fell on Feng Yuan and suddenly he stiffened.

We turned to look at her almost at the same time and found she was not her usual self. Her happy smile of a moment

出现在她脸上的轻松的微笑不见了，她的双眉紧锁，神情紧张，两眼盯着帐篷的入口，一动也不动，似乎是在凝神倾听什么声音。

“小冯，怎么回事？”我问道。

“我……我……”她的嘴唇颤抖着，“我好像听到帐篷外面有轻微的脚步声。”

“你一定听错了，”我说，“你也知道这附近一百多千米以内是没有人烟的，而调查队的同志全都在这帐篷里。”

“我没有听错。”冯元的眼睛里露出一种恐怖的神情，“吃晚饭时我在帐篷旁边丢了一个空罐头盒，刚才我甚至听到有一只脚踩在这空罐头盒上的声音。”

“说不定是只什么野兽跑到营地来了。”索伦说。

我走到帐篷门口，掀开挡布，用手电筒四处照了照，然而除了周围皑皑的白雪和似乎已经沉沉入睡的云杉林以外，既无人影，也不见兽迹。

冯元仍然执拗地摇摇头：“不是什么野兽，确实是人的

ago had disappeared; she was staring fixedly at the entrance of the tent, frowning with concentration as if she were listening intently for some sound.

"Feng, what is it?" I asked.

"I... I..." her lips quivered, "I seemed to hear light footsteps outside the tent."

"You can't have done," I said, "You know there's no human habitation for more than a hundred kilometres around here, and we are all here — there's no one else."

"I'm sure I did." There was fear in Feng Yuan's eyes. "I threw an empty can outside at supper time, round at the side of the tent, and just now I even heard a foot tread on it."

"Maybe it was an animal that came to our place," said Solon.

I went to the entrance and lifted the fly. I shone the torch in all directions, but I saw nothing except the vast expanse of white snow and the dragon spruce forest that seemed to have sunk into a deep sleep. There were no signs of human beings nor of animals.

Feng Yuan shook her head stubbornly and insisted: "It was not an animal—it was unmistakably the sound of

脚步声。”

索伦把头朝后一仰，哈哈大笑起来：“今天晚上你们是怎么了？首先是次仁旺堆，对于一段荒唐的传说将信将疑；现在又是你，居然听到了魔笛招来的山精的脚步声。我看是几个月来在这荒凉的环境里工作，已经开始影响到你们的神经了。”

“好啦，好啦，”我认为今天晚上对于这个题目的讨论已经够了，“夜深了，大家早点休息吧。”

第二天清晨，当我还在酣睡的时候，忽然被人急促地摇醒了。耳边有人低声喊着：“老王，老王！”

我睁开眼睛，发现是索伦在喊我。这时天刚刚黎明。从帐篷缝隙透进来的微光里，我看到他紧张的神色，立刻知道有什么意外的事件发生了。

“什么事？”我问道。

“老王，你快去看看！”

“看什么？”

“昨天小冯没有听错，帐篷外面是有……是有人来过，

human footsteps."

Solon raised his head and then gave a laugh. "What's the matter with you all tonight? First it was Comrade Ciren Wangdui half believing an absurd legend, and now Feng hears mountain goblins brought here by the magic flute prowling round the camp. I reckon working up here in this lonely place for several months has affected your nerves."

"Well, well!" I thought this discussion had gone on long enough tonight. "Comrades, it's very late. We'd all better go to bed."

Early next morning I was awakened from deep sleep by somebody shaking me vigorously and calling me in a low voice in my ear, "Wang, Wang!"

I opened my eyes and found it was Solon. The day was just dawning. From the faint light coming in through the fabric of the tent I could see he looked agitated. Something must have happened.

"What's the matter?" I asked.

"Wang, come quick and have a look!"

"At what?"

"Feng was right last evening. Someone really did come...

雪地上有脚印，”他又补充了一句，“可这是一种奇怪的脚印。”

“奇怪的脚印？”

任何人都看得出来，索伦这小伙子不是在开玩笑，而是严肃认真的。昨夜神秘的气氛似乎再一次笼罩了我，我钻出睡袋，迅速披上衣服，跟着索伦来到帐篷外面。

“你看！”他指着雪地说。

我低下头看了一眼，不知道是由于凛冽的寒意还是由于紧张，不觉打了一个寒战。

在雪地上，在昨夜我们自己践踏的脚印旁边，清晰地出现了两行脚印。这明显是一种两足动物的脚印，一左一右地排列。脚印分两行，一来一往，每一步的跨度在 40 厘米左右，似乎是一个用两足行走的生物异常谨慎地来到了帐篷门口，窥探以后，又走了回去。

我镇定下来，蹲下去仔细地观察了一番。这是赤足印在雪地上的痕迹，每个脚印长约 30 厘米，显示了一个短而宽的大拇指，不与其余四趾相并，而是单独向旁斜伸。

outside the tent. There are foot prints in the snow." Then he added, "But very strange ones."

"Strange ones?"

Anyone could see that the young man was far from joking now—he was very serious. Last night's eerie sensation gripped me again. I slid out of my sleeping bag and quickly scrambled into my clothes. Then I followed Solon out of the tent.

"Look!" He pointed at the snow at our feet.

I looked down... and shivered — the intense cold, or nerves?

In the snow, beside our own prints from the previous evening, were two distinct sets of footprints, evidently those of a biped, one left foot, one right foot. One set was coming and the other going away. The length of one pace was about 40cm. It seemed clear that a creature walking on two feet had very carefully come right to the entrance of our tent and then gone away again after having taken a peep at it.

I pulled myself together and squatted down to examine them carefully. They were prints on the snow ground made by bare feet. They measured about 30cm in length with the imprint of a broad and short hallux toe which stuck out sideways

其余的脚趾也很短，后跟圆而宽。从脚掌的细部来看，它有一定弧度的足弓，但又不像人类的那么明显。我立即判断出这不是人类的脚印，但又不是猿类的脚印，更不是其他动物的脚印。索伦的说法是对的，这是一组奇怪的脚印。难道山精真的出现了吗？

应当承认，冯元的听觉是十分敏锐的。就在离帐篷不远的地方，这个生物曾经踩在那个空罐头盒上，尖锐的铁皮可能划破了它的脚掌，所以在旁边还留下了几滴殷红的血迹。

这时调查队其他的人都已经起来了，大家看到这种奇怪的脚印以后，都面面相觑，不知道该怎么解释。

我们追踪着脚印，一直向山坡走去。脚印穿过我们帐篷旁边丛生的云杉，然后进入了一片灌木林，这里地面凹凸不平，而且枯枝很多，观察比较困难。出了树林，脚印便在坡地上一些裸露的花岗岩上消失了。看样子，它是从山上的密林中下来的。

我虽然不能解释这种神秘脚印的来历以及它和魔笛

instead of being in line with the other toes, which were also very short. The heel was broad and round. The indentation at the inner side of the print indicated some arch to the foot but not as much as on a human foot. I could see at once that they were not human prints, but neither were they those of apes or monkeys, nor of any other known animals. What Solon said was right: they were indeed strange prints. I wondered whether there were really mountain goblins?

We must admit that Feng Yuan certainly had sharp hearing. Just round the side of the tent a living creature had stepped on the empty can and the sharp tin plate might have hurt its sole, for a few red bloodstains showed up clearly in the snow.

By this time the others had got up. When they saw the strange prints they looked at each other in blank amazement, not knowing how to explain it.

We followed the trail which took us towards the slope. The tracks skirted the clumps of dragon spruces which overhung the camp and then entered a thicket of bushes. Here the ground was very uneven, with bumps and holes and a lot of layers of dead twigs, so it was rather difficult to see the trail, but once out of the wood we picked it up again, only to see it disappear on a bare granite slope. It seemed likely that it came down from the thick forest further up the mountain.

Though I could not explain the origin of the mysterious tracks, nor their association with the magic flute, I was aware

的关系，但是却知道这是一项极为重要的科学发现。这时东方的朝霞已经映红了雪山，而猛烈的山风也开始刮过了地面。为了保护这一珍贵的资料，我叫索伦选择了几组最清晰的脚印，绘图摄影以后，又浇注了石膏模型。就连罐头盒旁边的血迹，我们也连雪铲起，装进玻璃瓶密封起来。

接着，调查队的同志聚集在一起，商量下一步该怎么办。索伦主张在今天晚上再吹一次魔笛，同时埋伏几个人在树林里，看看来的究竟是什么东西。如果有可能，最好能捕获一个。“管它是人是鬼！”他最后还半开玩笑似地补充了一句。

“留下脚印的这个东西，自然不会是山精鬼怪，而是血肉之躯，是某种现在我们还缺乏认识的生物。”次仁旺堆推推眼镜，仍然是那样一本正经地说，“而且由于某种我们还不能解释的原因，它的出现和魔笛确实也有关系。根据我们调查队现在的人力和设备，要解决这个问题是很困难的。对待这种世界上罕见的科学现象，我们应当特别慎重，在缺乏进一步的研究和作出全面规划之前，我建议不要仓促采取行动，以免给今后的工作造成障碍。”

that it was a very important scientific event. As I pondered, the rosy dawn clouds in the east tinged the snow on the mountains with red and a sudden wind began to blow across the campsite. In order to preserve this precious evidence, I instructed Solon to select some of the clearest prints for measuring and photographing, after which plaster casts were made. We shoveled up the bloodstains by the can, together with some snow, and put them into a glass jar and sealed them up.

When these jobs had been done we got together to discuss what to do next. Solon suggested playing the flute again that evening while some of us kept watch in the forest to see who or what was coming. The best thing would be, he thought, to catch one if possible. "No matter whether it's a human being or a ghost," he added half jokingly.

"The creature which made those footmarks is definitely not a mountain goblin or a demon or a ghost; it's a flesh and blood creature, but it's one we know nothing about." Ciren Wangdui pushed back his glasses and went on as seriously as ever. "And for reasons which we can't yet explain, its presence is in some way connected with the magic flute. In view of our limited manpower and facilities we are probably not going to be able to solve this problem. We have encountered a rare scientific phenomenon in the world and we must be particularly cautious. I maintain that we should not take any hasty action until we have considered carefully and worked out a comprehensive plan, otherwise we may prejudice our future work."

我和大多数同志都同意这个方案。通过无线电与有关领导汇报以后，领导也支持我们的想法。就在当天下午，一架喷气式直升机在湖畔降落，将魔笛、手抄本、脚印的照片和模型以及血液的标本运到拉萨，并且立即转送到北京中国科学院的有关研究所去。

This was wise advice and most of us agreed with him. We briefed our headquarters about the matter over the radio and they approved our approach. In the afternoon of that day a jet helicopter landed on the shore of the lake and collected the flute, the parchment, the photographs and casts of the footprints and the blood sample which were flown first to Lhasa and then straight on to Beijing where they were handed over to the relevant institutes in the Chinese Academy of Sciences.

他们生存在 100 万年以前

三个月以后的一天，办公桌上电视电话机的蜂鸣器发出急促的“嗡嗡”的声音，指示灯标明了电话的来源地——北京。我按了按键，荧光屏上出现了一张两鬓斑白的中年男子的脸，他戴着宽边眼镜，穿着白色工作服，正亲切地然而似乎是略带疲乏地向我微笑。这个人的相貌，我感到有点熟悉，但是一时却想不起在哪儿见过他。

“王新同志吗？对不起，耽误你的工作了。”无疑他从荧光屏上看到了我手边堆积如山的书籍和稿纸。“我是朱苇。”

“朱教授，您好！”我高兴地说。现在我知道为什么觉得他有点面熟了，朱苇是全国闻名的人类学家，他的照片经常在报刊上出现。

朱苇点点头：“王新同志，你还记得三个月以前你们在天嘉林寺废墟上发现的魔笛和脚印吗？”

THE PIECES OF THE PUZZLE

One day three months later the buzzer of the TV telephone on the office desk gave out a rapid humming sound and the indicator showed that the call was from Beijing. I pressed the button and the face of a middle-aged man greying at the temples appeared on the screen. He wore broad frame glasses and a white lab. coat. He greeted me warmly but with a slightly weary air. There was something familiar about his appearance but I could not remember where I had seen him.

"Are you Comrade Wang Xin? I am sorry to disturb you." Evidently he had noticed the mountains of books and papers piled round me on the desk. "I am Zhu Wei."

"Professor Zhu, how are you?" I said excitedly. Now I knew why he looked familiar. He was a well-known anthropologist in China and photographs of him often appeared in the newspapers and magazines.

He nodded in response to my greeting and went on, "Do you remember the magic flute and the footmarks you discovered in the ruins of Tianjialin Temple three months ago?"

"当然记得，是您在负责研究它们？"说真的，虽然我们的考古调查工作已经初步告一段落，而且近来室内整理工作非常繁忙，然而只要稍有余暇，我总会回忆起有关拉布山嘉措神奇的传说。静静的月夜、魔笛的呜呜和令人难以置信的雪地上的脚印，并且尽力想要解释一下其中的奥妙，但是不论我从哪个角度考虑，都没有任何进展。这个无法解答的谜，日复一日地激起我强烈的好奇心，现在朱苇主动和我联系，我知道答案可能已经取得，我的心不由地猛跳起来。

朱苇简短地回答："是的。"

我的身后出现了沉重的呼吸声。我回头一看，冯元和索伦不知道什么时候悄悄地走过来了，满脸都是压抑不住的兴奋的表情。就连平常很沉静的次仁旺堆，这时也带着期待的神色站在一旁。

我将他们一个一个地向朱苇作了介绍。他向大家挥手致意："你们的名字，我都是熟悉的……"

朱苇的话还没有说完，冯元的问题就像连珠炮似地发

"Certainly. Are you in charge of the research work on them?" To be honestly, though we had preliminarily reached the end of one stage of our archaeological survey and I had been very busy classifying and writing reports recently at the office, whenever I had a moment I found my mind reverting to the mysterious legend of Lhabushan Jiaqu and to that quiet moonlit night when the eerie hooting notes of the magic flute somehow produced those incredible footprints in the snow. I tried my best and sought constantly for an explanation in one way or the other, but with no success. With this insoluble mystery in my mind, my curiosity grew stronger day by day. Now, with this call initiatively from Zhu Wei, I felt sure the answer was within reach. My heart beat fast.

"Yes," Zhu Wei replied concisely.

I was aware of someone breathing heavily just behind me. I turned my head back and found Feng Yuan and Solon had already come over quietly, unrestrained excitement in their faces. Even Ciren Wangdui, always quiet and controlled, was standing by with an expectant look on his face.

I introduced them to Zhu Wei one by one. He waved greetings to them, "I am familiar with all your names…"

Hardly had Zhu Wei really finished speaking when Feng Yuan bombarded him with questions: "What about the magic

了出来："那魔笛是怎么一回事？脚印究竟是什么动物留下的？它就是传说中的山精吗？"

看着这个性急的姑娘，朱苇教授的脸上又出现了那种疲乏的笑容："关于这些问题，我们已经有了一个初步的设想，但是这却不是能在电话里讲得清楚的。我今天和你们联系的目的，是想请你们尽快来北京一次，在有关的科学会议上介绍当时的实际情况，并且研究下一阶段的工作。正式的邀请函已经发给你们的单位。不知道你们的意见怎样？"

我回答说："天嘉林寺考古调查资料的整理工作即将告一段落，如果领导同意，我们可以来。"

索伦和冯元高兴地在我身边鼓起掌来，朱苇教授又被他们逗笑了："那太好啦，我等你们。"

"谢谢，再见。"

"再见。"朱苇的形象从屏幕上消失了。

科研单位的工作是非常注重效率的，领导很快就批准了我们去北京的计划。两天以后，我们一行四人乘飞机到

flute? What kind of creature made the footprints? Was it the mountain goblin of the legend?"

Professor Zhu Wei looked at Feng Yuan, who was showing a lack of patience, smiling with a weary air again. "As to those questions, we have some rough ideas but I can't tell you in detail over the telephone now. My reason for communicating with you today is that I want you to come to Beijing as soon as possible. You are to brief a scientific conference about everything that happened and then we can discuss the next step. The formal invitation has been sent to your unit. Now I want to know your opinion."

I replied, "The work of sorting out the collected archaeological survey material at Tianjialin Temple here is almost finished, so if headquarters agree, we can go to Beijing."

Solon and Feng Yuan were so jubilant that they clapped their hands by my side and Professor Zhu Wei laughed. "That's fine. I'm looking forward to your coming."

"Thank you. Goodbye."

"Goodbye." Zhu Wei then disappeared from the screen.

Scientific institutions take pride in being efficient and decisive and before long the authorities had approved our plan of going to Beijing. Two days later the four of us arrived

达了北京。

在科学院招待所安排了住处以后，我立刻给朱苇打了一个电话。

“你们来了，”他从荧光屏上向我打了个招呼，“明天上午九点，在我们研究所会议室，准备召开一次综合性的科学会议，请你们准时参加。八点半会有车来接你们。”

短短的两次电话，我已经感受到了这位科学家精干的作风。我压下了再提问题的想法，只是简单地说：“好吧！”

一句废话都没有，朱苇把电话挂断了。

第二天早晨九点钟，我们四个人出现在某研究所宽敞明亮的会议室里。参加会议的一共有二十多人，当我把这些代表的专业弄清楚以后，我才体会到朱苇教授所说的“综合性科学会议”的意义。原来这里面有人类学家、古生物学家、医学家、遗传学家、生理学家、无线电专家、雷达工程师、电视工程师……难道这一切都和解决雪山魔笛之谜有关吗？

朱苇教授从人群中认出了我们，他走过来亲切地和我

in Beijing by plane.

As soon as we had arranged accommodation for ourselves in the guesthouse of the Chinese Academy of Sciences, we promptly telephoned Zhu Wei.

"You've come!" He greeted me on the screen. "We plan to hold a multi-purpose scientific meeting in the conference room of our Institute at 9:00 tomorrow morning and you are invited to attend it on time. A car will pick you up at 8:30."

From the two short talks I had had with this scientist over the telephone, I had gained an impression of him as being very concise and capable. I resisted the temptation to ask questions and said simply, "All right. We'll be there on time."

Zhu Wei hung up without wasting time on further talk.

At 9 o'clock the next morning we entered the spacious, bright conference room of the institute. There were some twenty people present. When I found out what a range of specializations they covered, I saw what Professor Zhu Wei meant by "a multi-purpose scientific meeting". There were anthropologists, palaeontologists, medical experts, geneticists, physiologists, radio experts, radar engineers, TV engineers... Could they really have a part to play in solving the mystery of a magic flute in the snowbound Himalayan valley?

Professor Zhu Wei recognized us among the crowd of people and came over to shake hands with us. At close quarters

们一一握手。在近处观察，他似乎还要苍老一些，显得严肃一些。只有当他脸上浮现出我所熟悉的笑容时，才使人感到这是一位单纯的、平易近人的科学家。

“你们送来的数据，比我们原来想象的要复杂得多。在上级党委的领导下，我们组织了一个包括多种专业的联合研究小组，”他的手向到场的科学家们挥动了一下，“经过大家的协同努力，现在已经有了初步的结果。但是要彻底解开这个谜，却还要做大量的工作。这就是我们今天开会研究的目的。你的发言，安排在第一个，请准备一下。”

他来不及和我多谈，因为开会的电铃声已经响了。朱苇回到会议桌旁，宣布会议开始。

他简要地宣布了会议议程之后，满面笑容地对大家说：“现在，我们欢迎从拉萨专程赶来参加会议的王新同志发言。”

代表们热烈地鼓掌。我知道他们全都读过我写的情况报告，大致情况是清楚的。我先列举了各种有关拉布山嘉措的传说，描绘了天嘉林寺所处的环境、地形和周围动植

I thought he looked older and more solemn, but when the familiar smile appeared on his face his simple and genial personality reasserted itself.

"The data you sent us were much more complex than we had expected. We have organized a multi-discipline coordinating research group under the leadership of the Party Committee at the higher-up level." He waved his hand towards the scientists present. "Our combined efforts have achieved some results. However, if we want to solve the mystery completely, a great deal of work has yet to be done. This is the aim of our meeting today. You are to speak first, so please be ready."

Before I had time to reply, a bell rang to start the meeting. Zhu Wei went back to his place at the table and declared the meeting open.

Having told us the agenda, he said with a broad smile on his face, "Now let's ask Comrade Wang Xin, who has come from Lhasa to attend our meeting, to speak."

There was a ripple of applause as I stood up. I thought all of them must have read my report and were therefore clear about the general situation. I enumerated the various legends about Lhabushan Jiaqu first, described the surroundings of Tianjialin Temple and gave details of the terrain and of the flora and fauna of the area. Then I told them exactly how the

物群的情况，再详细介绍了魔笛的发现经过和手抄本的内容。大家都很感兴趣，听得十分专注。只有当我讲到索伦如何开玩笑吹响魔笛，而冯元听到脚步声以后又如何紧张时，会议室才爆发了一阵笑声。这使得冯元涨红了脸，感到很不好意思；而索伦首次出现了窘态，有点忸怩不安。

我讲完以后，又请次仁旺堆将他当时的推测作了一些补充。尽管他讲得很简短，措辞也很谦虚，但是看得出来，所有的代表对于这位藏族学者在事前产生的科学预感，以及事后处理这个问题慎重的态度，都是十分佩服的。

我们的发言结束以后，就轮到朱苇教授汇报研究的结果，也就是揭示这延续了几个世纪的神秘事件的内幕。会议室里鸦雀无声，所有代表的眼睛，都紧紧地盯着朱苇教授。我的手上原来拿着一支钢笔和一个笔记本，然而当朱教授用一种平静的声音开始讲述以后，我却忘记了记录，也忘记了周围的一切，而完全被他的讲话所吸引。在我们的眼前，展现了世界科学史上最为奇妙的、几乎是难以置信的一页。

flute was discovered and about the contents of the parchment. They listened with great interest and attention. When I described how Solon played the flute for a joke and how Feng Yuan was alarmed on hearing the footsteps, a laughter broke out in the conference room, which caused Feng Yuan's face to flush hotly, and also caused Solon to show signs of embarrassment for the first time and to feel somewhat blushing and ill at ease.

When I had finished, Ciren Wangdui added some supplementary observations and told the meeting about the opinions he formed at the time. His speech was short and the wording was modest, but it was clear that the Tibetan scholar had made a favourable impression on all the participants, both by his first scientific reactions and by the cautious attitude he took towards handling the problem afterwards.

When we had both spoken, Professor Zhu Wei began to tell the meeting about the results of the research and to unravel the centuries-old mystery. Silence reigned in the conference room. All eyes were fixed on him. I had a pen and notebook but as he spoke in a quiet, measured tone, I sat and listened with riveted attention, notes forgotten. I forgot all around me. He unfolded for us an account of a most wonderful and incredible page of the world's scientific history.

“关于拉布山嘉措魔笛的传说和这支魔笛发现的经过，以及它吹响以后带来的后果，刚才王新同志和次仁旺堆同志已经作了详细的说明。”朱苇教授说，“我们是科学工作者，是无神论者，当然不会用超自然的理由去解释它。这是一些表面上看来似乎是不可思议的神奇的现象，其中必然蕴藏着我们还未发现的某些自然界的秘密，我们就是怀着这个信念开始工作的。

“我们要解决的第一个问题，就是这些脚印究竟是什么动物留下来的。根据王新同志给我们送来的脚印的照片和石膏模型，我们仔细地研究了脚趾的形状、它们分布的位置、足弓的角度、脚跟的大小等细节，发现各方面的测量数据都介于人类和猿类之间。确切一点说，他们与大约100 万年以前生存过的一种直立猿人相近。大家知道，这种猿人比北京猿人还要原始，他的化石是近年来在康滇古大陆的一部分——四川西昌地区发现的。

“单纯根据一些脚印，当然是不可能作出确切的结论的，幸运的是，王新同志还给我们送来了一些血液的标本，

"With regard to the legends about the magic flute of Lhabushan Jiaqu, how this flute was found and the result of playing it, Comrade Wang Xin and Comrade Ciren Wangdui have just given us all the details," Professor Zhu Wei said. "We scientific workers are atheists and therefore, will not consider supernatural explanations. It must be possible for us to unveil what is hidden in these apparently mysterious and inexplicable phenomena. We started our work precisely from this conviction.

"The first problem we had to solve was what kind of animal left the footprints? From the photographs and the casts which Comrade Wang Xin sent us we have carefully studied the details of the shape of the toes and their alignment, the arch of the foot and the size of the heel. We found that the data from all these details indicated that the foot was somewhere between the human being and the anthropoid. To be more precise, it was approximately similar to the erect ape-men who existed on earth some one million years ago. As we know, these ape-men were more primitive than Beijing men (Sinanthropus pekinensis). Their fossils were discovered in recent years in Xichang Prefecture of Sichuan Province—which was part of the palaeocontinent of Kangtian.

"Naturally we could not draw accurate conclusions from the footprints alone. Fortunately Comrade Wang Xin had also sent us a blood sample. We conducted biochemical analysis

我们对血红蛋白α链上氨基酸的位置、血清蛋白朊等进行了分析，其结果都是和脚印的测定一致，这种动物应该属于高级灵长类，无疑具有介乎人和猿之间的特征。

“生存在100万年以前的、公认为早已灭绝了的一种猿人，居然到现在还有孑遗，这是可能的吗？带着这个问题，我们查阅了有关的文献资料，发现从战国时代开始一直到近代，有关康藏高原上野人的记载史不绝书。在两千多年的历史中，看到过野人的人很多，描绘也大致相同：身材高大，有棕色的毛。我们认为，这种记载中的野人，可能就是藏族传说中的山精，实际上就是那种在100万年以前生存过的猿人。

“在200万年到300万年以前，也就是地质学上的第四纪开始的时候，喜马拉雅山的上升运动虽然早已开始，但是总的说来，上升的速度比较缓慢，这一地区的地形仍然比较平坦，气候温暖适宜，森林密布，因此有猿人在这里出现，是一件很自然的事。大约从100万年以前开始，喜马拉雅山造山运动逐渐加剧，上升速度达到每百年1.2米到1.3米，

on the position of the amino acid on the α chain of the hemoglobin and the serum albumin protein, etc. and the results were identical with the determination of the footprints. This creature should belong to the higher primates and undoubtedly has features placing it between the human being and the ape.

"Is it possible that the kind of anthropoid apes which existed one million years ago and were universally considered to have become extinct long ago can still have descendants in this part of the world to this day? With this problem in mind, we consulted the relevant documents and data and found that from the time of the Warring States (475—211 B.C.) up to the present day there has been a steady succession of reports of 'wild men' on the Kangzang Plateau. During this period of more than two thousand years, many people claimed to have seen the 'wild men' and their descriptions of them were substantially the same: tall and sturdy with brown hair. We think that these 'wild men' might be the 'mountain goblins' of the Tibetan legends and that they are in fact the ape-men who existed a million years ago.

"About two or three million years ago—that is, at the beginning of the Quaternary Period—the ascending movement of the Himalayas, which had begun long before, was on the whole slow. The area was still comparatively flat with a mild climate and densely covered with thick forest, so it is naturally to be expected that ape-men lived there. Beginning about one million years ago the orogenic movement of the Himalayas gradually became more vigorous and the speed of ascent amounted to 1.2 to 1.3 metres per 100 years. As a result, the Kangzang Plateau became the highest

这就使现在的康藏高原，成了名副其实的世界屋脊。随着高度的增加，气候日趋寒冷干燥。崇山峻岭，冰雪覆盖。生活在这里的猿人，被迫向其他地方迁徙。不过在康格山深谷的温暖地带，在与世隔绝的原始森林中，却有一支猿人奇迹般地生存了下来，只是由于环境的孤立和生活方式的守旧，他们的体质和文化并没有再向前发展，而是基本上陷于停顿。他们可以说是在从猿到人过程中走入歧途、面临灭绝危险的一支。附带讲一句，像这种远古的化石动物在康藏高原复杂地形中残存的情况，并不是绝无仅有的，如曾经与猿人同时生活的巨猿和大熊猫，就都有后代存活到现代。”

讲到这里，朱苇教授停顿了一下，点上一支香烟。

性急的冯元是无论如何按捺不住了，她的声音打破了寂静：“朱教授，魔笛呢？那魔笛是怎么一回事？”

朱苇微微一笑，又继续讲了下去：

“这就是我们所要解决的第二个问题。魔笛和猿人究竟有什么关系呢？”

'roof of the world' in reality as well as in name. As it grew higher and higher, the climate became more severe and dry with each passing day. High mountain ridges were covered with ice and snow and the ape-men were forced to migrate to other places. However, in the warmer areas, like the deep valley of Mt. Kangga, ape-men were miraculously able to survive in primeval forest cut off from the outside world. Their physical constitution and culture remained basically static due to the isolated environment and a conservative way of life. We could say that they went astray from the mainstream of evolution from ape to man and thus they were on the verge of extinction. It is worth noting that this instance of ancient forms of life surviving to this day is not a unique case: the giant pandas and the giant apes that lived side by side with the ape-men in that remote period have their descendants living today."

Professor Zhu Wei stopped to light a cigarette.

Feng Yuan, unable to contain her impatience, broke the silence: "Professor Zhu, can you tell us about the magic flute? What does it do?"

Zhu Wei smiled and went on:

"That is the second problem we have to solve—what has the magic flute actually got to do with the ape-men?

“我们用录音机将魔笛的声音录下来,然后对现代生存的四种类人猿——大猩猩、黑猩猩、长臂猿和猩猩进行了试验。结果电生理仪器告诉我们，在听到这种声音以后，类人猿立刻产生条件反射，胃液、唾液分泌增多，并且顺着发声的方向寻找食物。而他们自己找到食物以后召唤同伴的声音，也大致和笛声相似。这就使我们有理由推测，拉布山嘉措的魔笛，实际上是模仿猿人觅食的声音而制造的，猿人听到笛声以后，以为这里有食物，自然就会应声前来。过去峨眉山寺庙的老僧呼唤猴群供人参观，也要模仿猴子的声音，这其中并无神奇之处。至于拉布山嘉措是怎么发现这个秘密的，当然我们不得而知。但是他是有意识地巧妙地利用了这一自然现象,为自己的迷信活动服务,这却是可以肯定的。两百多年来笼罩着天嘉林寺的神秘的色彩，原因也就在这个地方。

“那天晚上，当索伦开玩笑吹响了魔笛以后，可能有一个猿人正在帐篷附近，他听到这种声音，以为是同伴的召唤，于是悄悄地走到帐篷外面窥探，当他发现这里面

"We recorded the sound made by the flute and used it to conduct experiments on four kinds of anthropoids still in existence—the gorilla, the chimpanzee, the gibbon and the orangutan. Our monitoring instruments indicated that on hearing the sound these apes promptly reacted with reflex responses — their secretions of gastric juices and saliva increased and they went to look for food in the direction from which the sound came. Moreover, the sounds which they made to call their companions after they had found food was in many ways similar to the sound of the flute. Therefore, we have every reason to conjecture that Lhabushan Jiaqu's flute was actually made to imitate the sounds emitted by the ape-men while looking for food. When the ape-men heard the sound of the flute they thought there was food and would naturally go quickly in that direction. In the past the monks at the temples on Mt. Emei used this method to summon the local monkeys for the amusement of the visitors: they imitated the calls of the monkeys. So there is nothing mysterious or unusual about the technique. How Lhabushan Jiaqu discovered this secret we don't know, of course, but we can be sure that he made ingenious use of this natural phenomenon to deceive and delude the people into believing in his supernatural powers. That is why Tianjialin Temple has been shrouded in mystery for more than two hundred years.

"In the evening when Comrade Solon was playing the flute for a joke, an ape-man must have been near to the camp. It must have thought its companion was calling and stealthily peeped into the tent. When it found everything inside was

都是一些生疏的东西时，立刻警惕地退了回去。但是他的脚印却留在雪地上了。”

当朱苇教授讲完以后，会议室里一片激动的气氛，可以听到各种压抑不住的惊叹声。的确，就连我这个最早发现魔笛的人，听到事情竟然发展到如此出人意料的地步，也感到十分兴奋，不禁高声说道：“朱教授，这群猿人现在一定还在天嘉林寺附近，我们应该迅速组织调查队，立即寻找他们，这对于科学研究，该有多大的价值啊！”

“你的意见很对，今天请大家来，就是想初步讨论一下调查的方案。”朱苇教授说，“由于考古调查队的同志在发现脚印以后，采取了非常谨慎的态度，没有继续惊动他们，这就使我们的调查有很大成功的把握。根据上级党委的指示，要完成这项任务，必须运用最新的科学技术和先进的仪器设备，发挥社会主义的大协作精神。现在请大家发表意见吧！”

接着就是一场热烈的讨论。概括起来，各个方面专家

strange to it, it immediately retreated, alarmed. But it had left its footmarks in the snow."

When Professor Zhu Wei finished speaking, the atmosphere in the conference room was electric and people couldn't refrain from uttering words of admiring wonder. True, it was I who first discovered the flute but I still could not quite believe that I had started such an astounding train of events. In my agitation I found myself speaking to the professor:

"Professor Zhu, the ape-men must still be around Tianjialin Temple. Should we immediately organize a survey team to search for them? They must surely be of immense scientific interest?"

"You are right. Our reason for inviting you to come here today is to map out some such programme," said the professor. "The comrades of the archaeological survey team were commendably cautious not to alert the ape-men again after their discovery of the footprints. This will give us a better chance of success in our search. According to the directives from the Party Committee at the higher-up level, in order to accomplish the task, this project is to be carried out with the aid of the most advanced scientific methods and all the latest apparatus and facilities are to be made available. Complete socialist coordination is essential. Now, comrades, please state your views."

Heated discussion followed. To sum up, the views expressed

的意见归纳起来有以下几点：

生物学家的意见是，根据近年来对想要逃避人类侵犯的大型哺乳动物的观察，他们多半是夜出的，这就是说，白天躲藏和休息，晚上行动觅食。南亚的象群就是这样生活的。猿人在这样长的时间中没有被发现，很可能就是这个原因,因此专家建议调查队要将行动时间重点放在夜里。

电生理专家建议用电子仿真发声装置模仿魔笛的声音，再参考现代类人猿喜怒哀乐的各种表情加以变化，使它包含的内容更加丰富，根据不同的条件加以运用，引诱猿人前来。

雷达专家建议使用小型毫米波雷达,装置在密林深处,探索猿人的行动规律。

电视专家主张使用他们最新发明的自动变焦距红外线夜间摄像机，当猿人出现在预定地点时，就可以在荧光屏上进行实地观察。

声呐专家认为可以在安林湖畔广泛地空投一种简单而灵敏的声呐装置，它能自动分辨最轻微的两足动物的脚步

by the specialists in various fields were as follows:

The biologists pointed out that observations in recent years indicate that most of the large mammals that try to escape from the depredations of modern man are nocturnal, resting and remaining hidden by day and looking for food by night as, for example, the herds of elephants in southern Asia. This might explain why the ape-men had not been discovered before. They proposed, therefore, that the search team should work at night.

The electro-physiologists proposed using electronically synthesized sound to imitate the notes of the flute, with variations based on different moods of pleasure, anger, grief and satisfaction of the modern anthropoids. In this way a large repertoire of calls could be used in different circumstances to lure the ape-men.

The radar experts suggested that millimeter-wave radar be installed in the depths of the forest to detect the pattern of activities of the ape-men.

The TV experts were in favour of using their latest invention—a new infrared night vision camera with an automatic zoom lens. This would enable the observers at base to monitor the ape-men's activities on the screen when they appear on the predetermined location.

The sound people proposed that some simple and sensitive transceivers should be airdropped in the whole area around the shores of Lake Anlin. These transceivers could automatically pick up the faintest sound of the footsteps of a

声，并且向接收站发出信号，确定声源的位置。

一条一条的建议，一项一项的设想，逐渐形成了一个完整的作战方案。它显示了集体的智慧，社会主义科学大协作的威力。

biped and send signals back to the control station so that the position could be pinpointed.

All these suggestions and ideas gradually coalesced into a complete plan of campaign. It was a demonstration of the power of collective effort and socialist cooperation.

荧光屏上的奇观

我们的观测站设置在天嘉林寺废墟的经堂里，经过半个月紧张的筹备，仪器终于全部安置就绪。在旧日的佛龛上，装置着闪烁着红绿信号灯的操纵板，神怪的壁画前面，是大大小小的荧光屏。雷达和电视接收天线矗立在屋顶的经幡之上。于是，古老与现代、迷信与文明，在这里形成了强烈的对比，这可以说是世界上装备最为奇特的一座实验室了。

白昼已经消逝。在过去的十二个小时中，尽管我们不停地用雷达搜索着密林和山谷，但是除了丛林中常见的野生动物以外，没有发现异常情况，声呐装置也没有接收到大型两足动物的信号。看来生物学家的意见是正确的，猿人在白天没有外出，他们说不定正静静地躲在洞穴里休息。

定时器发出“嘀嗒嘀嗒”有韵律的声音，时间在流逝。虽然我们已经值了一整天的班，可是没有一个人愿意离开观察室，大家的眼睛，都盯在了发着淡绿色光芒的雷达

THE ASTONISHING ANSWER

Our observation post was set up in the lectorium in the ruins of Tianjialin Temple. After a fortnight's intensive preparation all the apparatus and instruments were in place. The control panel with winking red and green warning lights was set up on the old shrine, while the big and small radar and TV screens were in front of the mural of gods and spirits. The radar and TV antennae were mounted high on the pole over the Buddhist sutra streamers hanging on the roof of the temple. Ancient and modern, superstition and technology, formed a sharp contrast in what might well be described as one of the most peculiar laboratories in the world.

Daylight faded. In the past 12 hours we had found nothing extraordinary apart from the wild animals commonly seen in the forest despite continuous searching of the dense woods and valleys with radar. Neither did the transceivers pick up any signals from a large biped. It seemed probable that the biologists were correct and our quarry lay up in caves by day.

"Ticktack..." sounded rhythmically from the clock. Time was passing. We had been on duty all day but no one was willing to leave the observation chamber. All eyes were fixed

屏幕上。

二十二点。

二十二点三十分。

二十三点。

……

没有情况发生。

已经是午夜了，坐在我旁边的朱苇教授，摸出烟盒，点上一支香烟，默默地抽了起来。从他紧皱的双眉上，可以看出他在思索。而他所考虑的问题，应该是与我们每一个人所想的相同：难道我们的推测是错误的吗？难道我们的计划有什么漏洞吗？难道我们的行动不够小心，惊动了这群警惕性很高的猿人，使他们又迁徙到更深远的山谷里去了吗？

“朱教授，还要等下去吗？”冯元小声问。

“朱教授，是不是这群猿人的根据地在其他的地方？”索伦也不耐烦了。

没有回答。朱苇教授香烟头上的火光，急促地明暗着。

on the radar screen which glowed faintly green.

22:00.

22:30.

23:00.

…

Nothing happened.

It was already midnight. Professor Zhu Wei was sitting next to me. He pulled out a packet of cigarettes, lit one and smoked silently. He knitted his brows, lost in thought. We were probably all asking ourselves the same questions as he did: could we have made a mistake in our deductions? Could we have left something out of our calculations? Or had we been careless and alerted the ape-men having sharp vigilance with our operations so that they had moved away to some more remote valley?

"Professor Zhu, do we keep on waiting?" Feng Yuan asked in a low voice.

"Professor Zhu, could the ape-men's base be somewhere else?" Solon was also anxious.

No answer. The glow at the tip of Professor Zhu's cigarette intensified.

“同志们如果累了，可以先回帐篷去休息一下，”这是次仁旺堆平静的声音，“可是实验一定要坚持下去。我们要相信科学，相信科学的推理。”

“我同意。”朱苇教授斩钉截铁地说。

“注意！”俯身在屏幕前的雷达操作员失声叫了出来。

在不断接收着回波的雷达屏幕上，出现了一个光点。操纵员调整了一下旋钮，光点迅速变成了一个微微弯着腰的人形动物。

戴着耳机的声呐员警告似地举起了一只手。接着，从扩音器里传出了清晰的两足踏在积雪上行走的“簌簌”的声音。

“方位 150，距离 20 千米。”雷达操作员报告说。

微型电子计算机立即在立体地形图上标出了准确的位置，红色的指示灯亮了。

朱苇教授揉碎了手中的烟蒂：“在 B1 区。看来他们的营地是在康格山峡谷的深处。大家注意，实验开始！”

"Comrades, if you are tired you can go back to the camp and have a rest." It was Ciren Wangdui's quiet voice. "But the experiment must go on. We must have faith in science and the scientific deductions."

"I agree," the professor said firmly.

"Attention!" the radar controller, staring tensely at his screen, spoke sharply.

A light spot appeared on the radar screen that kept on receiving echoes. The controller adjusted the knob and the light spot immediately turned into a human-shaped creature with its waist slightly bent.

The sound controller wearing his headset raised his hand in warning. Immediately the crunching sound of a biped walking on the snow was clearly heard from the loudspeaker.

"Position: 150; distance: 20 kilometres," the radar operator reported.

The micro-computer plotted the actual location on the three-dimensional map and a red indicator light came on.

Professor Zhu crushed out his cigarette. "In B1 District. Their base is probably in the bottom of the gorge of Mt. Kangga. Stand by, everybody, the experiment now begins!"

他按了一下电钮。在 20 千米以外的一个预定地点，电子仿真发声装置发出了魔笛召唤猿人的声音。

电视机的屏幕亮了。虽然外面是漆黑的夜晚，可是由于新型的红外线摄像装置的作用，我们却清楚地看到，一棵棵盖着雪毡的高大枞树，像墙壁似地四面包围着一块空地。在通过电子效应重现的幽暗而苍白的光辉之下，景色寂静而又荒凉，这种情况与真实的夜景迥然不同，好像使我们追溯到若干万年前的岁月，回到了那遥远的古代。

魔笛的声音一再重复着。

“来了！”朱苇教授平静地说。

一丛灌木几乎微不可见地动了一下，一切又恢复了原状。虽然我们的观察室距离现场还有 20 千米，大家都知道猿人是无论如何也听不到这里的声音的，可是每一个人都紧张得连大气也不敢出，生怕微微的一点声息，轻轻的一点动作就会惊动那躲在灌木后面的生物。观察室里静悄悄的，只有仪器发出“嗡嗡”的声音。

朱苇教授调整了一下魔笛的音质，根据类人猿的习惯，

He pressed a button to start the electronic sound simulation transmitter broadcasting the sound of the flute, calling the ape-men to a predetermined spot 20 kilometres away from us.

The TV screen grew brighter. Though it was pitch dark outside, the newly developed infrared photography apparatus enabled us to see the tall snow-capped firs, like a wall encircling an area of open ground. In the pale, ghostly light produced by the apparatus the scene looked weird and, unearthly, utterly different from the actual night scene, as though we were looking back at an earlier stage of geological time in tens of thousands of years ago.

The "magic flute" sounded again... and again.

"Coming!" Professor Zhu said with composure.

A clump of bushes stirred very slightly and then everything was still again. We all knew that twenty kilometers away, where the ape-men could never hear us, but we all instinctively held our breath for fear that a light sound or a slight movement would alert the living beings behind the bushes. Only the faint humming of the instruments broke the dead silence in the observation chamber.

Professor Zhu made an adjustment to the tone quality of the electronic 'magic flute' so that it emitted the call that urged

这声音已经带有催促的意味了。

灌木又动了起来，枝叶逐渐地分开，出现了一个人形的脸，小心地窥探着。

魔笛又发出了一次声音，表示安全和满意。

终于，在观察站十几位望眼欲穿的科学家面前，第一次出现了大自然隐蔽了 100 万年之久的奥秘。一个人形的影子，慢慢地从灌木丛里钻了出来。开始是模糊的，然而随着他逐渐地走近镜头，形象就越来越清楚了。他的头上披着粗长的头发，除了脸部以外，全身都有茸毛。前额低平，向后倾斜，眉脊突出，鼻梁低而宽，下颌往后缩，脖子短而粗，整个头部向前伸，就像半低着头的样子。他的身躯十分强壮，两臂很长，相比之下，腿却很短，而且微微弯曲。他披着一块熊皮，一手持着一块拳头大的石制的刮削器。

猿人，这就是早已从自然界消失了的猿人，不是博物馆里根据几块化石复原的标本，而是活生生的实体。我的每一根神经都绷得紧紧的，我们正亲历着一个具有历史意义的时刻。

the ape-men to come together.

The clump of bushes stirred again and the branches and leaves slowly parted and a human-shaped face appeared. It peered out carefully.

The call of the magic flute indicating safety and satisfaction was broadcast.

At last, before the riveted gaze of some dozen scientists in the observation chamber, one of nature's well-kept secrets was revealed in its true form for the first time in a million years. A shadow in a human-shaped form slowly broke through the bushes and came out into the open. At first it was hazy but as it came into focus the details grew clearer and clearer. The hair hanging down from its head was coarse and long and its body was all covered with hair except for its face. The forehead was low and flat and inclining backward, the superciliary ridge was prominent and the bridge of the nose low and broad. The lower jaw sloped straight back to the neck which was short and thick. The head was thrust forward in a half lowered position. The body was robust with very long arms and, by comparison, very short legs, somewhat bowed. It wore a bear skin and was holding a stone scraper as big as a fist in its hand.

It was an ape-man, the ape-man who had disappeared in nature so long ago and who was here before us, real and solid, not the specimen reconstructed from a few fossils in a museum. I was tense with the realization that I was experiencing a moment of historic significance.

猿人并不知道有这么多双眼睛在注视着他的行动。他慢慢地走到空地中央，一路上不停地左顾右盼，保持着高度的警惕，似乎一有风吹草动就准备逃走，然而黑夜仍然像帷幕似地掩护着他，周围仍然是死一般的寂静，他显然放心了。

在空地中央，我们有意识地堆放着一些粮食和牛肉。猿人发现了这么丰盛的食物以后，显然十分兴奋，他回过头去，发出了一种低沉的、音节分明的声音。

“语言，”我听见次仁旺堆轻轻地对朱苇教授说，“猿人是有语言的。”

“是的。”朱苇教授回答，“从他的行动来看，他们已经习惯夜间行动，这证明他们的视觉和嗅觉是发达的。”

随着这个猿人的召唤，丛林中又出来了几个猿人，有男的，也有女的。他们看到了食物以后，脸上都流露出惊喜的表情，互相用那种低沉的语言交谈着，还做着生动的手势。的确，这群长期和严峻的大自然进行生死搏斗的猿人，在隆冬的季节，能找到如此精美的食物，真是一件

The ape-man, unaware of course of being the object of such concentrated attention, slowly walked to the centre of the open ground, keeping a sharp lookout in all directions as it went. It behaved as if it was ready to escape at the rustle of a leaf in the wind, but the darkness and the dead silence around it evidently reassured it.

Some grain and beef had been intentionally put in the centre of the clearing. The ape-man was very excited when it found this prize. It turned its head over its shoulder and uttered a low syllabic sound.

"Language." I heard Ciren Wangdui mutter to Professor Zhu Wei. "They have some language."

"Yes," said the professor. "And from their behaviours, they must be accustomed to moving about at night: their senses of sight and smell are evidently highly developed."

Following the ape-man's call, several others, male and female, came out from the bushes. On seeing the food they looked pleasantly surprised and talked to each other in low, deep voices using lively gestures. Certainly to have found all this food in the depth of winter was an exceedingly happy

非同寻常的大喜事啊!

在对他们进行了比较细致的观察以后，在场的科学家们已经无法抑制自己的激动，开始七嘴八舌讨论起来了。

“你看他们的手，大拇指已经很发达，和其余四指分得很开，这已经不是猿的前掌，而是和人手基本相似了。”

“是的，你再注意那脊椎骨的形态，这已经比猿类要挺直得多，而他们的腿也比猿类要直一些。”

“看到他们手中握的刮削器没有？这是用石片打制成的。我国的旧石器时代文化，从它的早期阶段开始，就有着共同的性质，这就是主要使用石片石器，而少用石核石器。像北京周口店中国猿人遗址、周口店第十五地点、丁村旧石器时代遗址等处都是这样。这种猿人的时代比北京猿人还要早，这就证明使用石片石器的传统，比我们过去想象的要早得多!”

“还有他们披的熊皮上有烧焦的痕迹，这证明他们已经能够使用火了。”

“大家的意见都是正确的。”荧光屏前响起了朱苇教

event in their ceaseless struggle against the harshness of their environment.

After an initial period of absorbed observation, the scientists on the spot could no longer contain their excitement and all began to talk at once.

"Do look at their hands. The thumb is well developed and the other four fingers are clearly separated. That is no ape's fore-paw—it's much more like a human hand."

"That's right. And do you see the line of their spines? They are much straighter than apes' spines and their legs are straighter and longer too."

"Did you notice the scrapers in their hands? They are made of slate. All the Old Stone Age sites in China had a common characteristic in its early stage: slate vessels were mainly used rather than pebble stone ones—Beijing man had them at the 15th Site in Zhoukoudian and they were found at Ding Village, the ruins of the Old Stone Age—and now we know the tradition of using scrapers dates back much earlier than we had thought: these ape-men came long before Beijing man."

"The scorch marks on the bear skins show that they use fire."

"Comrades, your views are correct," Professor Zhu's voice

授的声音，这是我第一次发现这位冷静的科学家内心蕴藏着如此充沛的感情。“总的说来，他们已经能够制造工具，能够劳动，因此，他们已经不是猿，而是属于人的范畴了。劳动创造世界，劳动创造了人，这一伟大的真理，现在又一次得到了确切的证实。同志们，我们现在所看到的，并不是简单的自然现象，而是自然辩证法的胜利，是马克思主义理论的胜利啊！”

朱苇教授的心情，我是能理解的。自从1859年英国生物学家达尔文发表《物种起源》一书，提出生物界进化论的观点，1863年赫胥黎发表《人在自然界中的地位》，明确提出人是由猿猴进化而来的看法以来，在一个多世纪中，关于人类起源的问题，争论很激烈。尽管近十年来古人类化石的发现日益增多，研究日益深入，但是比之于1000多万年以来从猿到人无比丰富的历史内容，我们所掌握的资料仍然是非常贫乏的。现在我们的眼前竟然有一群活着的猿人，他们是沟通猿和人之间的环节，他们的体质构造、生活习惯和社会组织，都为我们复原了一幅幅100万年以前

cut through the babel in front of the TV screen. It was the first time I saw this sober-minded scholar betray his natural enthusiasm. "Broadly speaking, they can make tools and can perform tasks, therefore, they are no longer apes but ape-men. Labour has created the world; labour has created mankind. Now, here before our eyes is further conclusive proof of these great axioms. Comrades, what we are observing is not just a simple, natural phenomenon but the triumph of natural dialectic, the triumph of the theory of Marxism!"

I could understand the professor's feelings. Since Darwin, the British biologist, published his book *The Origin of Species* in 1859 which set forth his theory of evolution by natural selection and Huxley published his work *Man's Place in Nature* in 1863, in which he explicitly expounded his view that man evolved from the anthropoid ape, there have been heated controversies over the origin of mankind for more than a century. Despite the discovery of increasing numbers of fossils of the ancient hominids and the intensification of research into the subject in the past ten years, the data available to us comprise a very meagre spin-off from the history of more than ten million years during which man was evolving from the ape. Now we had a group of living ape-men who were a link between the ape and man. Study of their physical characteristics, their way of life and their social organization would help us to restore lively pictures of life that existed more than a million years ago. The great scientific

发生过的生动的画面，这在科学上的重大意义，是能用言语表达的吗？

兴奋和喜悦的浪潮，淹没了我们每一个人。如果不是在观察站里，我相信我们是会欢呼起来的。

就在我们讲话的时候，猿人们已经扛上了粮食、牛肉，慢慢消失在密林深处了。但是这些朴实的大自然的儿女哪里会知道，在粮食和牛肉中，我们都装置了微型无线电发射机，根据电波再去追踪他们藏身的洞穴，那只是一件非常简单的事了。

我的故事到此马上结束了，至于以后我们怎样用同样的方法找到了全部残存的猿人部落，怎样将康格山建设成一个人工保护区，让这些猿人自由而幸福地生活，同时也向我们提供了大量珍贵的科学资料，以至于全部从猿到人的历史，不得不作重大的修改和补充，这些都是你们所熟知的事，我就不多啰嗦了。

significance of these events could not be expressed with words.

We were overwhelmed, every one of us, with excitement and a sense of achievement. If we had not been in the observation chamber we would have cheered.

While we were talking, the ape-men gathered up the food and slowly disappeared into the depths of the forest. However, these primitive sons and daughters of Mother Nature would never know that we had put micro-transmitters in the food. It would be easy for us to locate their caves in accordance with the electric waves.

My story ends here. How we found all the remaining tribes of ape-men with the same method later on and how Mt. Kangga has been made into a conservation area in which the ape-men live freely and happily, while at the same time providing us with a great deal of precious scientific data so that the history of evolution of man from ape-man is being substantially revised and supplemented — all this is well known and I do not, therefore, propose to repeat it here.

作者简介

童恩正（1935—1997），湖南宁乡人。考古学家、科幻作家。1961 年毕业于四川大学历史系考古专业，先后在峨眉电影制片厂、四川大学工作和教学。1991 年，赴美讲学，后移居美国。在美期间，他曾担任匹茨堡大学和多所大学的教授，成为美国知名教授之一。

1957 年发表第一部作品，1960 年开始从事科幻小说及科普作品的创作。其作品《珊瑚岛上的死光》被评为中国科幻小说重文学流派代表作，曾多次获奖，并曾在 20 世纪 80 年代初期被拍摄成电影，是我国第一部科幻电影作品。

曾任四川省政协常务委员，中国科学文艺委员会主任委员。

About the author

Tong Enzheng (1935—1997) was a native of Ningxiang, Hunan Province. Tong was an archaeologist and a SF writer. Graduated from Archaeology Faculty of the Department of History at Sichuan University in 1961. First worked at Emei Film Studio and then taught in Sichuan University. Invited to give lectures in the USA in 1991, and afterwards he migrated to the United States where he had served as professor for University of Pittsburgh and several other universities in succession. He had become a well-known professor there.

His first literary work came out in 1957, and in 1960 he began to write SF and popular science works. His work *Death Ray on the Coral Island* was regarded as the representative work of the school of SF laying particular stress on literature. It had won a number of prizes and was made into a film in the early 1980s. It was the first SF film in China.

Tong had been a standing member of the Chinese People's Political Consultative Conference of Sichuan Province, and a director member of China Science and Literature Commission.

译者简介

温绍贤　生于香港，早年毕业于中山大学西方语言文学系。温绍贤是资深翻译家和中英文编辑，翻译和译审的书籍超过 100 部；他还是长期从事英汉语言比较和翻译研究的学者，有多部学术专著问世；他同时又是小说作家，擅长撰写政经历史长篇小说，代表作有《红的回忆》五部曲和“绿印人”系列三部短篇小说集。现任郑州大学西亚斯国际学院荣誉教授。

在中国图书对外推广网和中国作家协会共同建立的“翻译名家”和“作家档案”网上，均有介绍温绍贤的条目。

有关温绍贤生平的详情，请参阅网上“维基百科”对他的介绍。

英文文字编辑简介

蒂娜·巴莱（Tina Bailey），资深英文译审。

About the translator

Wen Shaoxian was born in Hong Kong. He graduated from the Department of Western Languages and Literature at Sun Yat-sen University. He is a veteran translator as well as a professor of translation and comparative grammar. He has translated and copy-edited more than 100 books of different disciplines.

Now Wen is also a literary writer, expert in writing political and historical novels. His representative works include *Red Memories* pentalogy and *New Immigrants*, a series of three short story collections. Now Wen is honorary professor at SIAS International University in Central China.

About the English copy–editor

Tina Bailey, veteran English copy-editor.